AN ARCHITECT'S DILEMMA

CREATING SYSTEMS WITHOUT LOSING THE SOUL

ARUN KUMAR CHOKKAPPA

An Architect's Dilemma

ISBN 978-93-344-4286-1
First published in 2025
TEACHING TAURUS

This book is self-published by the author, Arun Kumar Chokkappa, under the Imprint TEACHING TAURUS.

This book is a work of non-fiction. The views and opinions in this book are the author's own, drawn from personal experience and extensive reading. It is intended as a philosophical suggestion or professional guidance. Readers are encouraged to consult an expert before making lifestyle changes. The author affirms that no content is intended to offend or discriminate against any person, entity, religion, caste, gender or region.

Illustrations were created by the author using Adobe Firefly AI generator. Any resemblance to real individuals or entities is purely coincidental. This book is a legacy offering, ritualized with emotional clarity and symbolic stewardship.

Cover Design and Typesetting by Pen Bird Designs

Cataloging in Publication Data--DK
Courtesy: D.K. Agencies (P) Ltd. <docinfo@dkagencies.com>

Chokkappa, Arun Kumar, 1980- **author.**
An architect's dilemma : creating systems without losing the soul / Arun Kumar Chokkappa.

pages cm
Includes bibliographical references.
ISBN 9789334442861
1. Conduct of life. 2. Self-realization. I. Title.

LCC BJ1589.C46 2025 | DDC 170 23

CONTENTS

Hands that held the Thread vii

Echoes of the Thread xiii

The System's Vocabulary xix

Letter to My Dear Reader xxi

Prologue xxiii

1. Designing Systems without losing the soul 01
2. Reflection on System Design, Intention and the Actor-Observer Dynamics 11
3. Tension between Ethical Design and Ego Driven Systems 21
4. Internal Ethics to the System they inhabit 31
5. How to design Systems with Intention? 41
6. Ethical System Design 51
7. Personal Leadership and Legacy 61
8. Legacy Design and Mentorship 71
9. Observer's Compass 81
10. Daily Clarity Practices and Reflections 91
11. A Call to Clarity and Legacy Imprint 101

Epilogue 112

Recommended Readings 113

Choice is already made for You,
Your purpose is to understand the
WHY behind it

Hands that held the Thread

This book has been less a solitary act than a journey walked with many companions. Each step carried echoes of encouragement, patience, and quiet trust.

I owe a special debt of gratitude to Group Captain S Ramesh VM (Retd) – a decorated Indian Air Force officer, awarded with the Presidential Award for meritorious service, whom I first met 32 years ago at Sainik School Amaravathi Nagar. Looking back, I can see how profoundly he has inspired me- through his witty humour, his serious philosophy, and his example of leadership. As I completed my manuscript, he was the one I turned to, and our late-night discussions went far beyond revisions of the text. They become memories in themselves, shaping personal philosophies and ideologies that continue to guide me. A simple 'thank you' cannot capture the depth of my appreciation for this inspirational leader. I remain humbled yet confident, grateful to have found in him not only a mentor but a brother I can always reach out to. His presence gave me confidence when the path seemed uncertain. His reminders helped me hold back when I wanted to push too quickly, and in that restraint, I found rhythm.

I am deeply grateful to Professor Dr Sanjay Andrew Rajaratnam, my teacher in physiology, whose influence has extended far beyond the classroom. What began as conversations around doubts in physiology soon grew into discussions on music, books, and personal support. He has been a lighthouse not only for me but for countless students, guiding with wisdom and generosity. Over the past 28 years, he has remained my go-to person, always giving his time readily-including his thoughtful review of this manuscript.

I am grateful to Ms Chital Mehta, once my colleague, with whom I had only limited interactions until I discovered her gift for writing. Reading her works of fiction opened the door to exchanges that grew richer over time. I have been awed by her transformation from a software engineer to a full-time writer, which also included a master's degree in creative writing in the U.S. The scale she has reached since then in the world of literature is remarkable. Her latest work, 'Have you seen Romit?', which won the James Alan McPherson Prize (2025), stands as a testament to her talent and dedication. Despite achieving such heights, she readily gave her time to review my manuscript and share her feedback. That generosity inspires me as much as her journey itself has inspired me to write. For her support and for the example she continues to set, I remain deeply thankful.

I extend my sincere gratitude to Dr Ashvin Varadharajan, MBBS (AFMC), Research Fellow at Washington University in St. Louis, for generously dedicating his time to reviewing my manuscript. His discerning eye and thoughtful feedback reflect not only his eye for detail but also his remarkable acumen for research. I deeply value his contribution, which has enriched the work.

My Heartfelt Thanks to Ankur Warikoo, best-selling author of Do EPIC Shit, entrepreneur, coach and mentor to millions of youth. Since 2022, I have been following his work – sharing my thoughts on LinkedIn, watching his YouTube sessions, and even attended one of his WebVeda Courses. Through these interactions, I found myself resonating deeply with his way of approaching life and work. During my writing journey, one of his posts struck me profoundly: " If you don't ask, it's always a No." It made me realise how often I had shied away from asking, and it gave me the courage to reach out to him with my manuscript. To my surprise, he responded with a simple note – "send when ready" – and a thumbs up. That moment reminded me to keep my work going, no matter the doubts. When I finally completed my manuscript, I shared it with him, still sceptical if he would find the time. Yet again, he surprised me. True to his word, he read it and gave me his feedback. That gesture made me realise why he is a leader who truly walks the talk. His generosity left me humbled and gave me an added sense of responsibility to ensure this book carries the care and clarity.

Mr Gowsihan, of Pen Bird Designs, the silent man who resonated with me to bring the book into its form. His patience and quiet strength carried the layout from idea to completion. In his silence, there was clarity; in his resonance, the manuscript took its shape.

I am what I am today, and the language is yet to have a word that I can use to say it all to my parents for giving me the foundation to stand on, my wife for bearing with my eccentricities and still hanging on, and my kids for everything.

My friends, though I hardly call, who remain in my memory and continue to support me in their own quiet ways: Thank You !!!!

Together, they held the thread that carried this book into being.

"A profound guide for anyone trying to build systems that serve rather than suffocate, blending clarity, ethics and inner awareness. Arun invites you to design a life with purpose, humility and a compass that never loses its North."

- Ankur Warikoo

Bestselling author of DO EPIC SHIT,

Entrepreneur, Speaker

Echoes of the Thread

"It is well written and compiled
empowering its readers to reflect and learn the rhythm of life."

- Prof.Dr. Sanjay Andrew Rajaratnam,
MD (Physiology)

"An Architect's Dilemma is a much-needed read for our times. Arun has emphasised the need to pause, reflect, and design systems that work for us as individuals. This book is a true guide for anyone seeking peace, clarity, and meaningful choices as they navigate life's challenges."

- Ms Chital Mehta, Author - 'Have you seen Romit?'
James Alan McPherson Prize Winner (2025)

"Systems, we do inherit. If inheritance is left static, it is bound to stale or stagnate. System Enhancement is nothing but everyone's duty and a show of gratitude; An Architect's Dilemma is a reveille towards realization for the current generation submerged in virtual slumber. In pondering over system building, Arun has, in many subtle ways, touched upon the ethical and philosophical points of view, which will awaken you within."

- Group Captain S Ramesh VM (Retd),
Indian Air Force

"A beautiful piece of writing that is sure to make timeless concepts of structured living and personal organization accessible to it's readers through simple analogies and engaging illustrations"

- Dr Ashvin Varadharajan, MBBS (AFMC),
Research Fellow at Washington University in St. Louis

Dedicated to
My Parents, Wife, Kids, Teachers, Mentors, Friends
And the inner Architect

"Sit where you will... The reflection decides whether you are an Architect, Observer, or Actor."

The System's Vocabulary

Architect

1. a person who is qualified to design buildings and to plan and supervise their construction.
2. a person who is responsible for inventing or realizing a particular idea or project.
3. a person who designs hardware, software, or networking applications and services of a specified type for a business or other organization.

Observer

1. a person who watches or notices something.

Actor

1. a person whose profession is acting on the stage, in films, or on television.
2. a participant in an action or process.

Dilemma

1. a situation in which a difficult choice has to be made between two or more alternatives, especially ones that are equally undesirable.
2. a difficult situation or problem.

LETTER TO MY DEAR READER

Dear,

I did not write this book to be read.

I wrote it to be remembered – silently, in moments of confusion, clarity or choice. This guide is for those who feel systems pressing in, but still choose to act with care. For those who get pulled to the question – What am I building and why?

It is for the architect who does not yet know they are designing every day. Whether you are 17 or 70, if you have ever felt the tension between clarity and conformity, this is for you.

Let this book be a mirror
Let it breathe
Let it serve

Arun Kumar Chokkappa

PROLOGUE

To the Quiet Architects

Most systems you walk through were built before you arrived. School, Career, Culture, Identity. They whisper scripts. They reward performance. But they rarely ask you to pause.

But beneath the noise, there is a quiet voice.
It does not shout, it observes.
It does not chase, it designs.
That voice is yours.

This guide is for those who feel the tension between clarity and conformity. For those who sense that something is off – but do not know how to name it.

For those who want to build, but not bend the rules.
Lead, but not grip.
Teach, but not mold.

You are the architect – because every choice shapes a blueprint
You are the observer – because clarity begins with reflection
You are the system designer of your own rhythm – because only you can align structure with the soul

This book will not give you answers. It will provide you with mirrors. It will offer questions, metaphors, and quiet tools. It will help you navigate the matrix without getting overwhelmed by it.

Whether you are in high school, college, or early in your career, this is your invitation to build with clarity, live with detachment, and leave a legacy that breathes.

Let's begin....

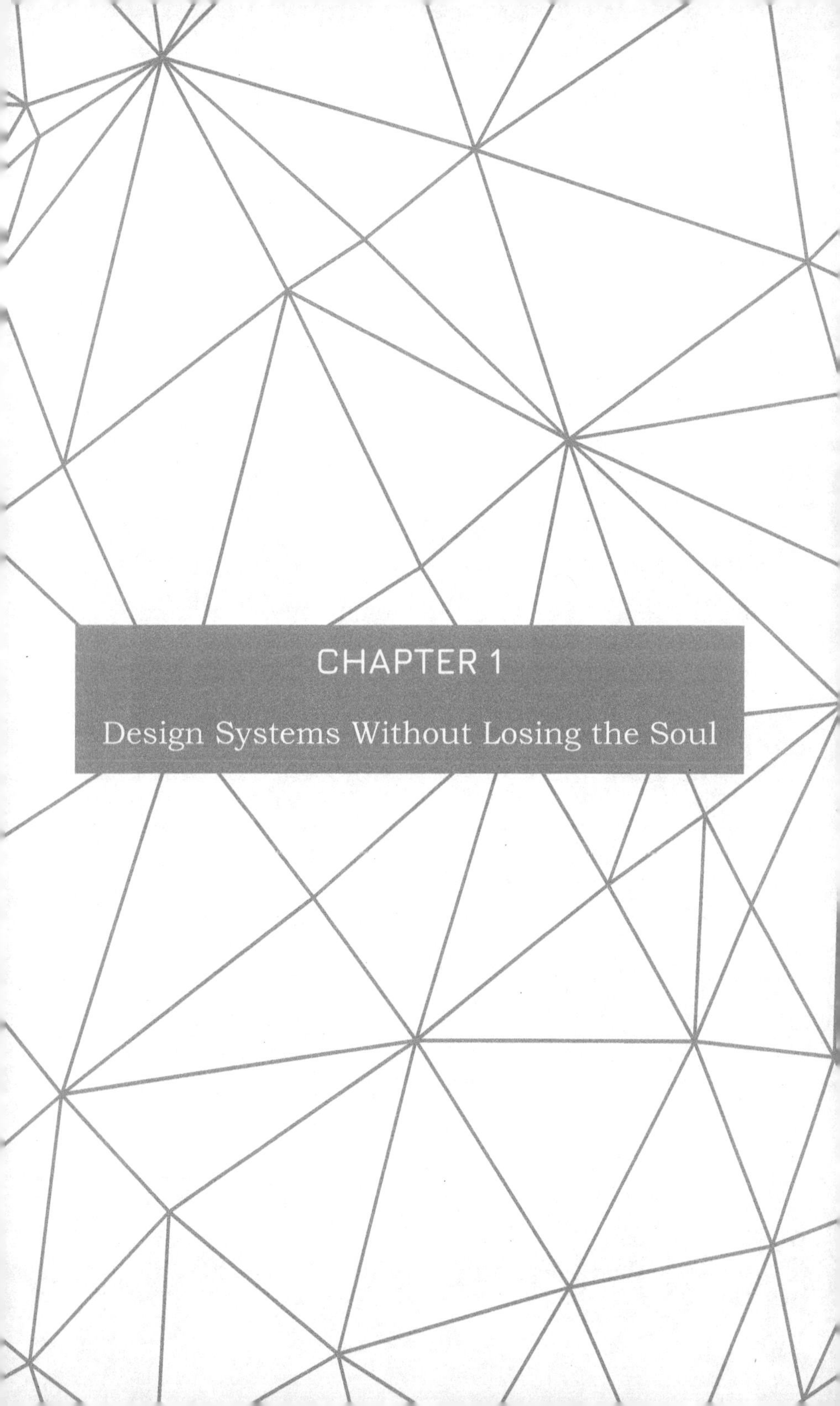

CHAPTER 1

Design Systems Without Losing the Soul

You were born into systems - but you were meant to shape them with clarity , core and courage

ARCHITECT AWAKENS

When chaos surrounds. Awakening begins within.

Every society builds systems. Schools, Law, Rituals, Careers.

They give structure, rhythm and shared meaning.

Without systems, Chaos!

With too much system, Stagnation!!

We have all experienced these crowded systems where rules seem more important than meaning. Confusion arises when control takes precedence over care, leaving us lost in the noise. Awakening begins the moment we choose clarity over chaos.

The awakened Architect is there to design, not control, but to support life flow, because design fosters the flow of life while control stifles it.

IS THE ARCHITECT, GOD?

We have all stood in the fog of systems – Clarity is choosing design over disorder.

Some say the architect is God. Others say it's another actor. Either way, the system must be built.

Each one of us face moments where systems feel bigger than us – school rules, office politics, family expectations. Confusion arises when ego or fear drives the design, leaving us trapped within.

Awakening begins when we see the architect not as God, but as ourselves choosing clarity.

But if the architect designs with ego or fear, the system bends towards control.

Ethics dissolve when outcomes dominate intention.

COLLECTIVE THOUGHT SUSTAINS PROCESS

Process breathes through trust and not control.

Systems thrive when built on shared clarity – not obsession with results.

When people act with purpose, the process flows.

Just like a team project that advances when voices align, but stalls when everyone seeks credit.

Families thrive when purpose is shared, but disintegrate when control overshadows care.

When they chase outcomes, the process fractures.

The architect must trust the collective, not micromanage it.

THE ACTOR AND THE OBSERVER

Clarity comes when the actor remembers the observer within.

The actor performs. The Observer watches.

But they are one.

The observer creates the actor, then guides it.

If the actor forgets the observer, it gets lost in the Matrix (Maya). If the observer controls the actor, it becomes the Matrix.

A student chases grades, forgetting the quiet voice that asks, "What am I learning?"

An employee pursues recognition, while the observer whispers, "Does this align with my values?"

When actor and observer walk together, life flows with balance instead of confusion.

DESIGNING WITHOUT ATTACHMENT

Freedom in design begins where attachment ends.

To design ethically is to let go. The architect must build with care, then release control. Systems need to breathe.

The observer stays still.

Because only in stillness can the actor move freely without bending the process.

A parent guides a child, not to control the future, but to nurture growth.

A leader shapes a team, not to chase credit, but to sustain.

Peace arrives when design serves life, not the attachment.

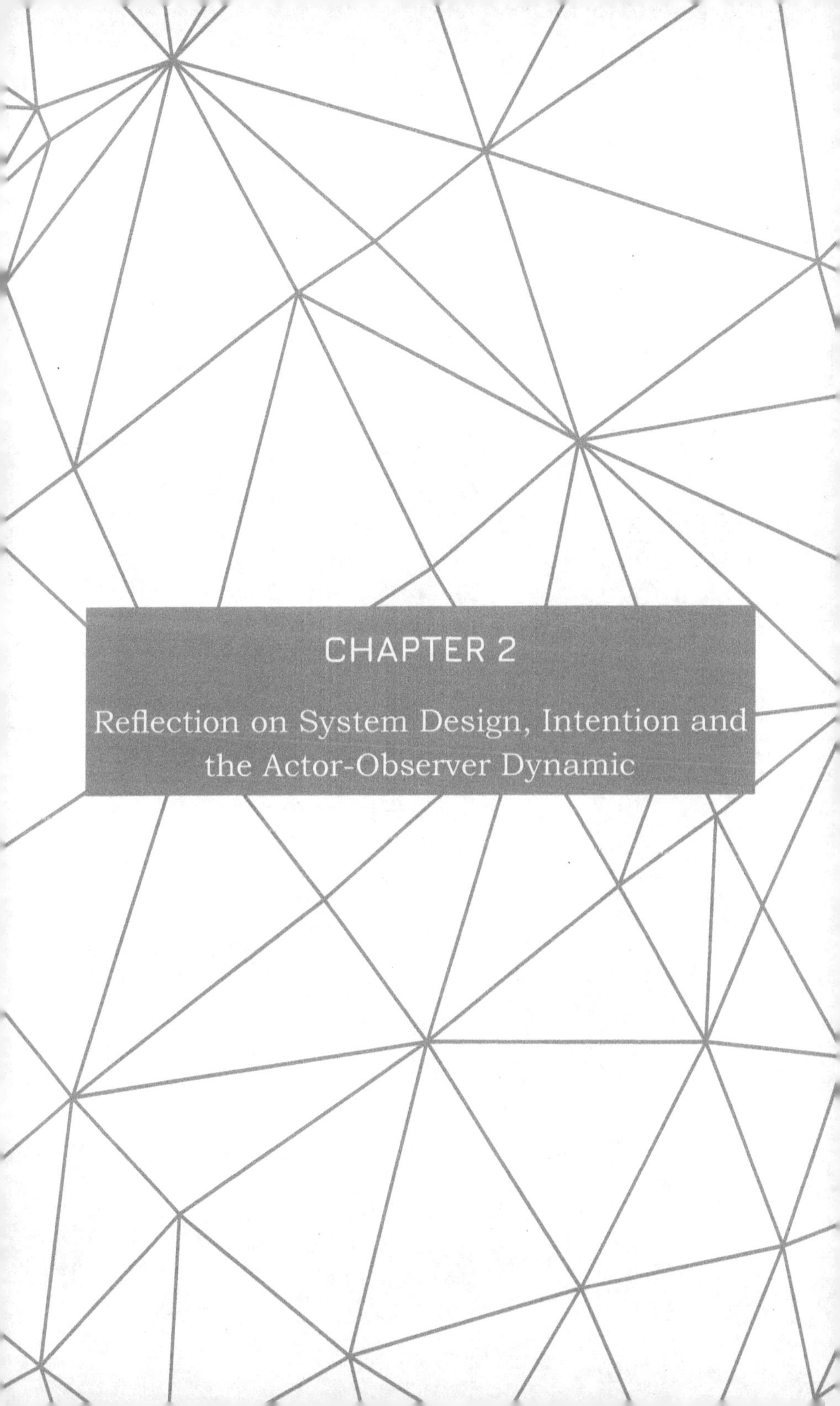

CHAPTER 2

Reflection on System Design, Intention and the Actor-Observer Dynamic

Before you design the system -
observe the self that wants to design

THE SYSTEM MUST EXIST

Like a gardener, the architect trusts the system to grow.

Without systems, we drift. Without structure, even good intentions scatter. The architect's first duty is to create form, not control, but for coherence.

A gardener sows the seed, then steps back to let nature breathe. Just waters with care, not with obsession, trusting the rhythm of growth. Life flourishes when nurture replaces control, and the process is left to unfold.

A system is not a cage. It is a rhythm.

But rhythm must never become rigid.

WHEN ARCHITECT BENDS THE PROCESS

The act pauses… the observer bends,and the process falters.

When the architect obsesses over results, the process wraps.

Metrics replace meaning. Control replaces clarity. The system begins to serve itself, not the people.

Ethics fade when the process is no longer trusted.

These are moments when architect needs to pause before the act. Just like how a trusted friend at work urges you to remember the space for ethics and trust in the process. Yet, when the intention to push forward overtakes, the rhythm bends.

THE OBSERVER'S ROLE IN DESIGN

The observer empowers by giving space, not by showing every move.

The observer must guide the architect – not with control, but with awareness. The observer sees the long arc, the quiet consequences. It reminds the architect: build with care, release with trust.

Systems need to breathe.

A coach steps aside, letting the kids play the game themselves. Resisting the urge to show every kick, allowing them to learn through play. Growth comes when guidance steps back and the system allows discovery.

THE ACTOR'S TRAP

The actor's crown is only an illusion.

The actor wants results. Wants recognition. Wants Speed. But when the actor designs without the observer, the system becomes a mirror of the ego.

The trap is subtle: the actor believes it's building for others, but it's indeed building for itself.

A man reflects on himself to be a king. He mistakes the symbol of reality, forgetting the system that gave him the role. The trap is not the crown itself, but the blindness that confuses power with truth.

DESIGNING FOR LEGACY AND NOT CONTROL

Legacy is not possession, but continuity; the house is his voice, the grandson its continuity.

Legacy is not control. It is continuity.

The architect must design systems that outlive EGO, outlast trends, and outgrow their creator. This is ethical design: not to dominate, but to serve. Not to impress but endure.

Just like how a grandfather narrates the story of the house he built to his grandson. He does not dictate how it must be used, but shares the values it represents. True legacy is not control over tomorrow – it is the gift of meaning that endures.

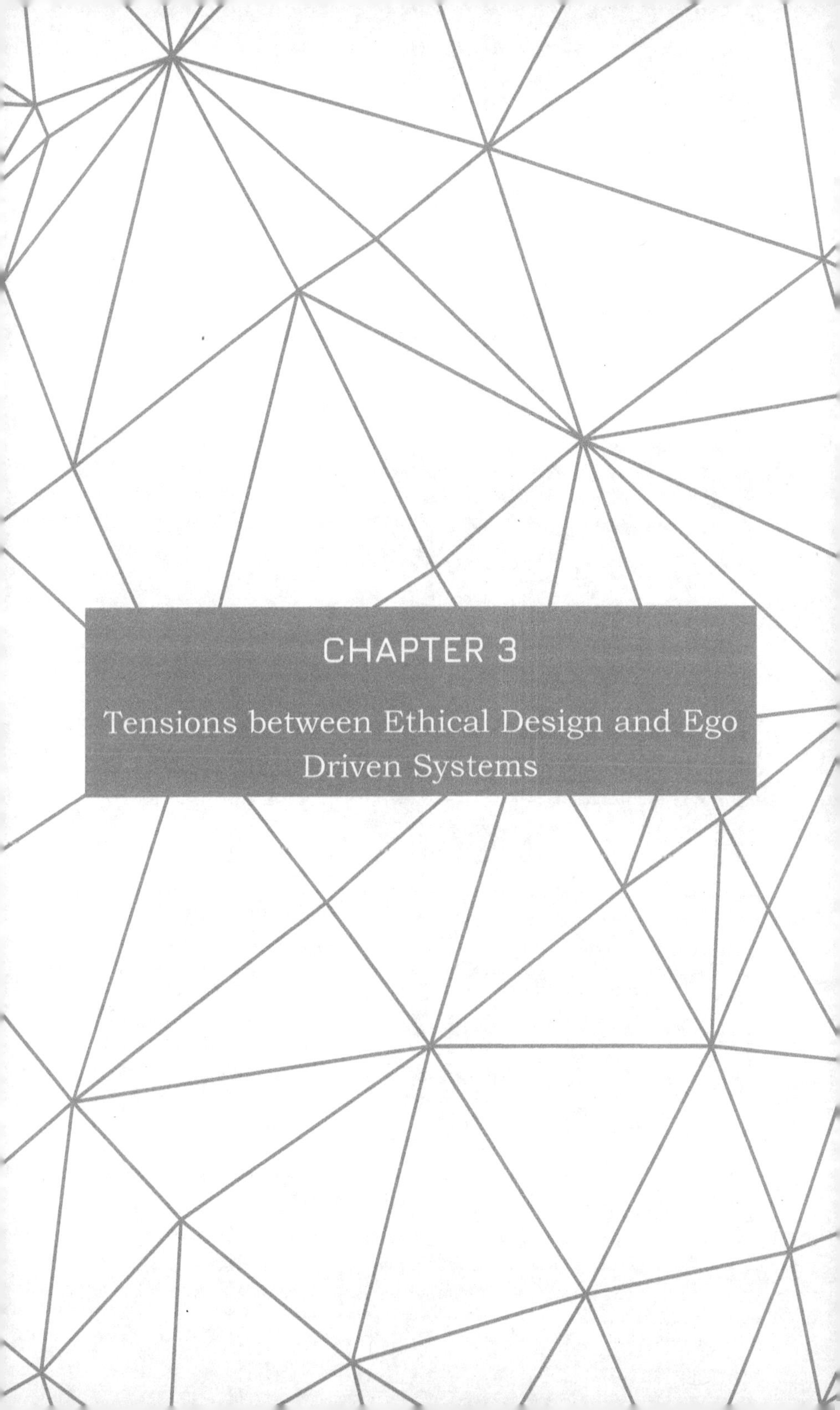

CHAPTER 3

Tensions between Ethical Design and Ego Driven Systems

When ego enters the blueprint, clarity fades. Design must begin with humility

SYSTEMS THAT FORGET

Systems that forget purpose become monuments to emptiness.

Some systems forget why they were built. Schools chase grades, not learning. Hospitals chase billing, not healing.

The architect must remember: systems are tools, not truths.

How many times have we stopped by the schools and hospitals, asking why they were built at all? We remember they were meant to awaken minds and heal bodies, yet now they only serve the routine. The buildings remain, but their spirit is gone – systems that forget their purpose become hollow shells of what they once promised.

EGO IS THE BLUEPRINT

Invisible care sustains the system.

When the architect designs to be remembered, the system forgets its purpose. EGO sneaks into the blueprint through complexity, control and legacy chasing.

The best systems are invisible.

They serve quietly and dissolve when no longer needed.

A mother adds salt to a meal, never boasting of its necessity. She serves her children with quiet devotion, never seeking applause. The system endures when its blueprint is cared for without ego – seen in results, not in display.

Without salt, food is bland; with ego, systems lose their flavour.

THE OBSERVER'S SILENCE

The deepest design is consciousness observing its own action in silence

The observer does not interrupt. It watches. It waits. It speaks only when the actor forgets the script. In system design, silence is wisdom. The observer reminds the architect:

Build for flow and not for fame.

A man works, yet within him another presence quietly watches. His own consciousness observes the action, not to judge, but to reveal clarity. The silence is not external – it is the inner witness that makes the actor aware.

THE ACTOR'S URGENCY

In the age of likes, urgency becomes performance, not purpose

The actor wants speed. Wants impact. Wants applause. But urgency bends ethics. The Observer must slow the actor down-not with force, but with clarity.

Systems built in haste often collapse in silence.

Youngsters post every detail of their day online, chasing instant approval. Each action is hurried, not for its value, but for the reaction it might bring. The actor's urgency is a trap of our times – doing and showcasing everything, while forgetting why it mattered in the first place.

DESIGNING FOR THE UNSEEN

The seed sown today becomes unseen fruit for tomorrow's generations.

Design for those who will never thank you.

For outcomes you will never witness. For clarity that outlives your name. This is ethical architecture: invisible, intentional and free from the need to be seen.

An old man sows seeds and nurtures a small plant. He knows he may never eat its fruit, yet he takes care of it with devotion. Years later, the tree grows tall, feeding generations who never saw the hand that planted it. Designing for the unseen is the quiet act – giving without expectation so others may reap it's benefit.

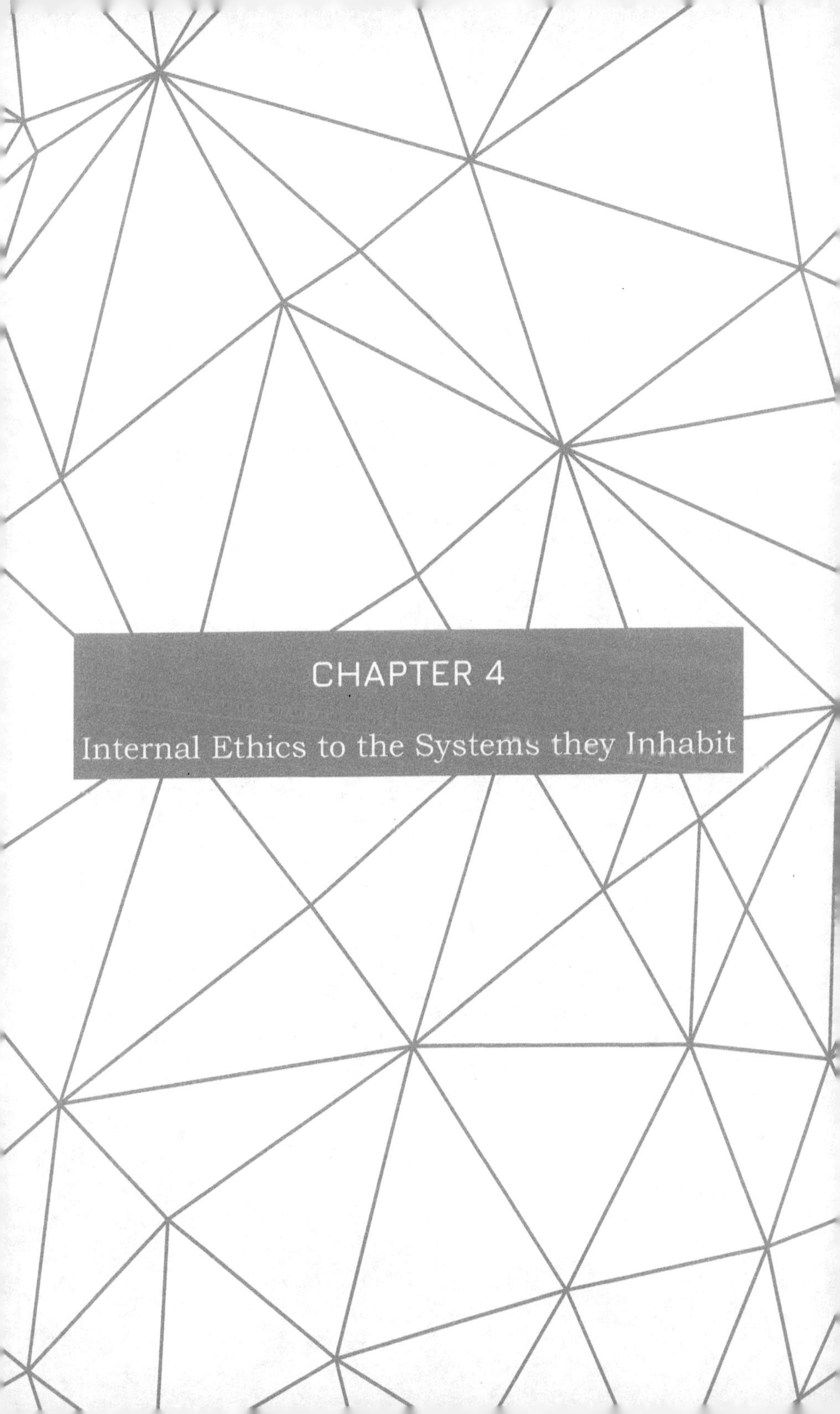

CHAPTER 4

Internal Ethics to the Systems they Inhabit

> You did not choose the system - but you can choose how to walk through it

SYSTEMS WE INHERIT

What we live becomes what they inherit.

Most systems weren't built by us. We inherit them – school, family, culture.

The architect may be long gone, but the design remains.

To live ethically is not to reject the systems, but to observe them, question them and reshape them when needed with care.

A father runs beside his son, silently watching. He sees his own traits reflected in the boy's stride – joy, discipline and rhythm. He feels both happiness and responsibility, knowing inheritance is not only genetic but acquired through action. The father realises: systems we inherit are shaped not by words, but by the life we live before others.

SCHOOL AS A MATRIX

Perplexed by grades, the boy wonders – what does this matrix of school truly mean?

Grades... Ranks... Rules... School teaches structure-but sometimes forgets meaning.

The actor chases marks.

The observer asks: 'What am I learning about myself?'

Education must be more than performance. It must awaken the architect within.

A boy sits in class, staring at the report card. He sees grades, targets, and completion, but none of them explain why he is here. The system tells him to achieve, but not what it means. He goes blank, realising that school has become a matrix – numbers without purpose, measures without meaning.

CAREER SCRIPTS

Atop the career ladder – he wonders if success was his choice – or the system's script.

Get a degree. Get a job. Get promoted.

The script is loud. But scripts are not the truth.

The observer must ask: Is this my rhythm or someone else's? The actor performs. The observer chooses when to rewrite.

A man stands at the peak of his career, celebrated as a high achiever. He followed the pattern, grades, promotions, milestones – each step scripted by the system. Now at the summit, he pauses. The applause is loud, but the question is louder – Was this truly his path, or the system's inheritance?

He realises that systems we inherit are not only genetic-they are cultural, professional, and invisible scripts that shape our lives..

IDENTITY LOOPS

In the loop of likes, many mistake applause for identity.

Social media, Labels, Expectations – They loop identity.

The actor wants likes.

The observer wants the truth.

When Identity becomes performance, the MATRIX (Maya) deepens. To be free is not to reject identity but to hold it 'Lightly'.

Youngsters post their lives online, waiting for the flood of likes. Each notification feels like proof of who he is. But as the loop repeats, he drowns- believing identity is what others acknowledge, not what he discovers within.

The system of identity becomes a trap; external applause replaces inner awareness.

THE QUIET ARCHITECT WITHIN

Within him, the architect watches the actor – wearing the observer's hat, guiding the purpose.

Every person carries an architect inside.

Not Loud. Not Famous.

Just quietly designing a life of clarity. The observer watches. The actor moves. Together, they build systems that serve – not control.

This is the beginning of ethical design.

A man works at his desk, focused on the task. Yet within him, another presence quietly watches – not just observing, but shaping. This is the architect within, wearing the observer's hat, ensuring each action aligns with the larger design. The actor performs, but the architect safeguards purpose, silently weaving meaning into motion.

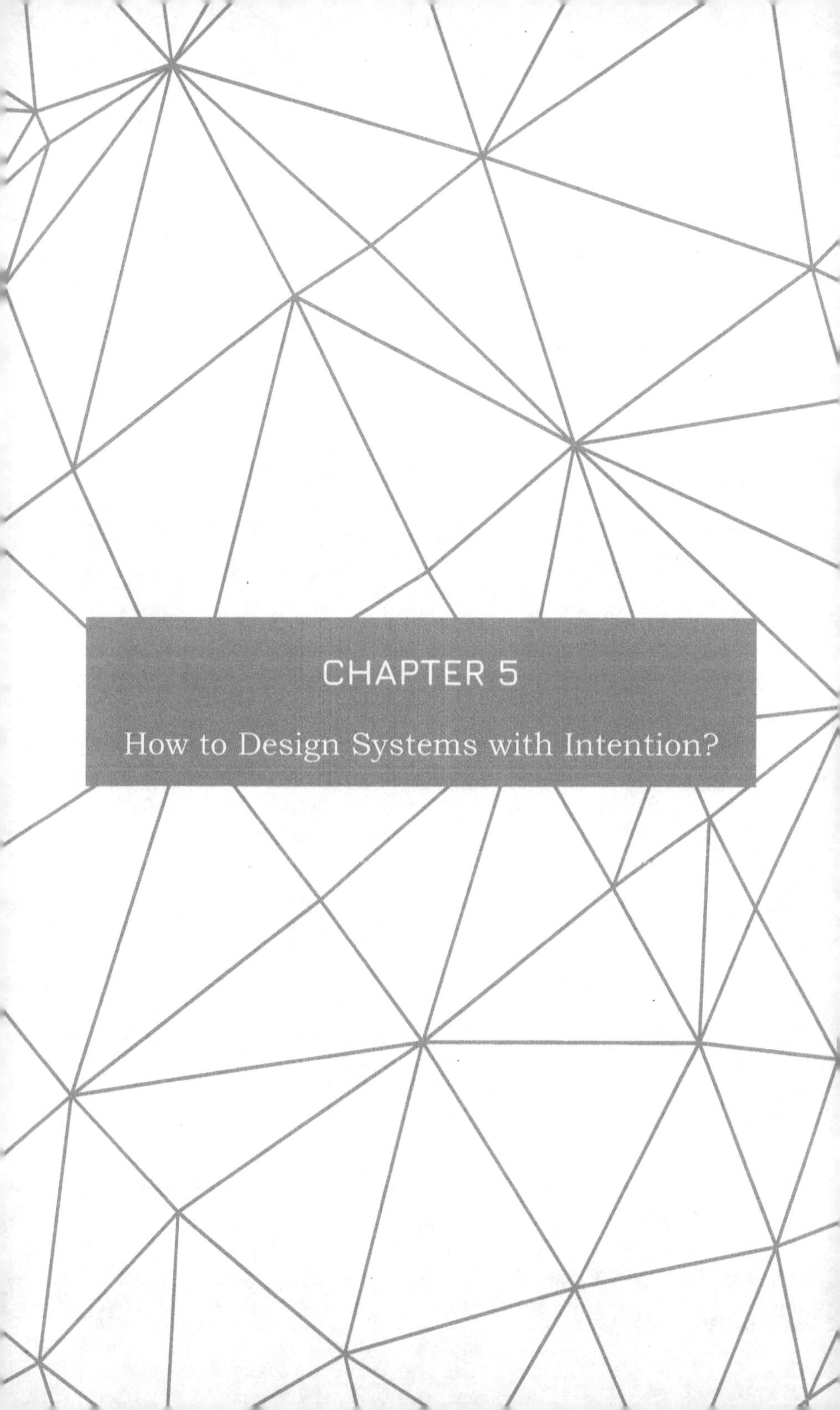

CHAPTER 5

How to Design Systems with Intention?

Every System begins with a question.
Every legacy begins with intention

SYSTEMS WE BUILD

Trends sip into us – systems are built by what we imitate.

Not all systems are inherited. Some we build routines, friendships, projects, and teams.

Every choice is a design.

The architect within you is always working.

The question is: are you building with clarity? Or just copying old blueprints.

Two friends are in a cafe sitting by a vending machine. One chooses a cola that's in trend, the other picks a different flavour. Yet, as they chat, the second friend reaches for a sip of the trendy cola. In that moment, a system is built – not by inheritance, but by imitation. Systems spread not through force, but through the quiet pull of what seems accepted.

We inherit some systems, but we build others – often without knowing why.

DESIGN BEGINS WITH INTENTION

Every system begins with a seed of intention.

Before you build anything, ask: Why? Not what will I get? But what will this serve?

Intention is the seed.

If it's clear, the system will grow with integrity. If it's cloudy, the system will bend towards confusion.

A young engineer contemplates his assignment in urban development. Intention became his compass. He chose to design spaces that respected community, blending progress with care.

THE ETHICS OF SIMPLICITY

The straight road reminds simplicity is the cleanest ethic.

Complex systems often hide confusion.

Ethical design is simple, transparent, and kind.

The observer asks, "Can this system be understood by those it serves?" If not, it's not ethical. Simplicity is not weakness – it's wisdom.

A walk along a straight road that has no curves to confuse, no detours to mislead; we will realise that simplicity is not weakness – it is strength, and ethics lie in keeping things simple, clean and clear.

Complexity confuses; simplicity clarifies.

DESIGNING WITHOUT EGO

The quietest work endures-the loudest collapses.

Designing with EGO means building for applause.

Designing with clarity means building for service.

The actor wants to be seen. The observer wants the system to work – even if no one knows who built it.

The young boy poses beside an ancient bridge, taking a picture. The bridge has stood for centuries, carrying countless lives across. Its designers never thought of fame or applause; they worked with intent, not ego. Today, the boy's photo is proof of their legacy – a design that endures beyond recognition.

SYSTEMS THAT HEAL

Hospitals heal today; colleges prepare healers for tomorrow.

Some systems hurt. Others Heal. The difference is INTENTION. A healing system listens, adapts, and respects those within it. You can be the architect of healing – at home, in school, in teams.

Build with Care.

Let the systems breathe.

A hospital stands as a sanctuary for the sick, thriving with experts who dedicate themselves to healing. Over time, it evolves into a medical college, where knowledge is passed on and new minds are trained. The system adapts – healing is no longer just about treating patients, but about preparing future healers. This is a metaphor of systems that heal: they do not stop at cure, they expand into continuity, ensuring care for generations.

CHAPTER 6

Ethical System Design

> To design is to shape experience. To do so ethically is to begin with humility

DESIGN IS A RESPONSIBILITY

Design serves when it eases burdens – responsibility lives in humility and not applause.

To design anything – a team, a habit, a classroom- is to shape experience.

That is a responsibility, not a reward. The architect must ask: 'Will this serve others, or just reflect me?'

Ethical design begins with humility.

A high-profile professional notices an old woman struggling with her trolley suitcases. She steps forward, helping her cross the road. The wheels on the suitcase, designed with care, already make her burden lighter. Her act of support completes the design's purpose – not for selfies or recognition, but for service.

FEEDBACK IS PART OF THE DESIGN

Feedback is the spoonful that makes the whole meal right.

No system is perfect.

Feedback isn't failure – it's refinement. The ethical architect listens, adapts and improves. To ignore feedback is to build a wall. To welcome it is to build a bridge.

In a kitchen, a mother prepares soup for her family. Before serving, she offers a small portion to her daughter. The daughter's response guides her – too salty, too bland or just right. This feedback ensures the meal is not only cooked, but perfected. Every household thrives on this system: feedback is part of design, part of care, part of legacy.

Design without feedback is flavour without taste.

THE POWER OF INVISIBLE DESIGN

Invisible design carries the journey – unseen, yet unforgettable.

The best systems often go unnoticed.

They work quietly, support gently and dissolve when no longer needed. The architect doesn't need to be credited.

The system doesn't need applause.

Impact is enough!

A passenger boards a train, enjoying the comfort of the ride. He notices the scenery, the rhythm, the ease of travel. What he does not notice are the wheels and racks beneath him – meticulously designed, tested, and perfect. They remain invisible, yet they are the very reason the journey is possible. This is the power of invisible design: it creates impact without demanding recognition.

LEADERSHIP WITHOUT CONTROL

True leadership hands over, creating space for systems to thrive beyond self

Leadership isn't control – it's clarity.

The ethical architect leads by example, not by force. They create space, not pressure. They guide without gripping. That's how systems stay alive.

The captain of the team with a black wrist band stands next to his team member holding the trophy. He knows that leadership is not about holding, but about releasing. By stepping back, he creates space – a system that will remain alive even when successors take his place. This is leadership without control: guiding without grasping, empowering without possession.

LET THE SYSTEM BREATHE

Less baggage, more comfort - systems breathe best when kept simple.

Every system needs space to evolve.

Overdesign suffocates. Under design confuses.

The architect must balance structure with freedom. Let the system breathe. Let the people within it grow.

On a railway platform, a young lady is seen with minimal luggage, just what she needs for her travel. Her journey is lighter, freer, more comfortable. She realises that the same is true for systems: when they carry too much baggage -rules, complexity, clutter – they suffocate. But when they are kept simple, they adapt and endure.

Systems breathe when we let them be light.

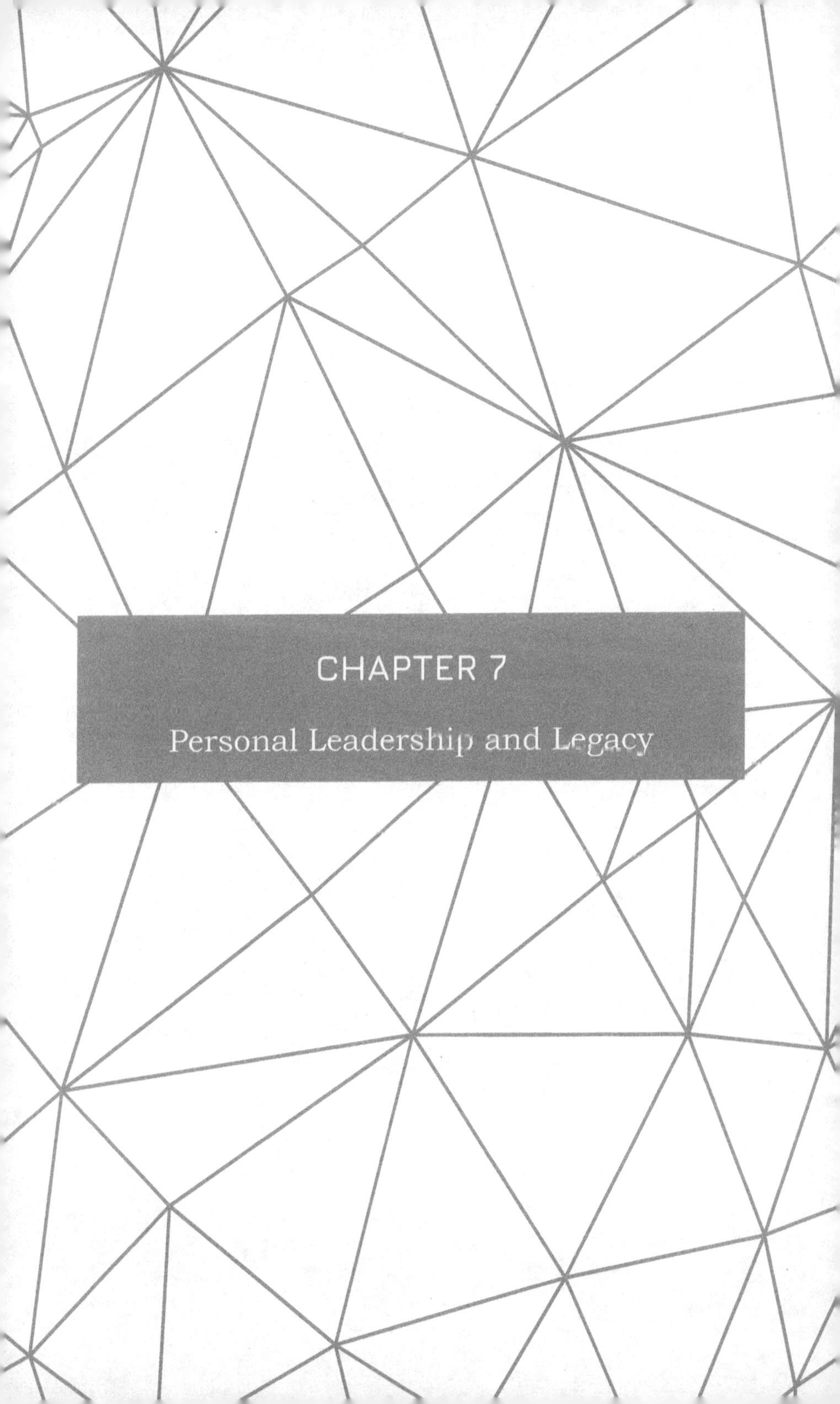

CHAPTER 7

Personal Leadership and Legacy

Legacy isn't built in moments - it's shaped in choices, quietly, consistently, and with care

SYSTEMS ARE MIRRORS

Systems reflect their creators – mirrors of intent, values and legacy.

Every system reflects its creator. If built with fear, it controls. If built with trust, it follows. The architect must look inward before designing outward.

What you build is a mirror of what you believe.

A man stands before a mirror, seeing his own reflection. Systems are no different when observed: they reveal who built them. A system of fairness reflects a fair mind; a system of confusion reflects a confused one. By examining a system, we gain insight into its creator – their intent, values, and vision.

THE MATRIX CAN'T TOUCH CLARITY

The web of the matrix cannot bind a mind that sees with clarity.

When the actor moves with clarity, the MATRIX (Maya) loses power. Systems may distract, distort or delay - but they cannot touch the observer.

Clarity is immunity.

It is not an escape. It is present.

A young adult stands before a spider web. The web is intricate, designed to catch and hold. Yet his vision is clear – he sees beyond the illusion. The matrix cannot touch him, because clarity is stronger than complexity.

Systems of confusion collapse when met with the light of clarity.

THE ACTOR MUST BE SUPPORTED

An actor thrives when guided by design and reflection, not by applause alone.

The actor is not the enemy. It's the part of you that moves, builds and serves. But it must be supported by the observer without reflection, the actor burns out without action, and the observer fades.

Balance is legacy.

On stage, a young girl performs. Her father watches closely, observing her movements. Her mother mirrors a gesture, showing her how it could be refined. Together, they provide the feedback she needs – not criticism, but support.

The actor cannot grow without the architect's design and the observer's reflection. Systems endure when actors are supported, not left alone.

LEGACY IS QUIET

Roots and Shoots remind us – legacy grows quietly, yet endures beyond time.

Legacy is not loud.

It's not fame, wealth or applause. It's the quiet impact you leave in systems, people and moments. The ethical architect builds for those who may never know their name – but will feel their clarity.

A seed rests in soil. Roots sprout downward, unseen, anchoring life. A shoot rises upward, defying gravity, moving silently. This quiet feat is nature's legacy – created without noise, sustained without applause.

Noise fades; legacy grows in silence.

THE SYSTEM IS NOT YOU

Roles belong to systems; identity belongs to you.

YOU are not your job, your grades, your role or your system. YOU are the observer who creates, guides, and lets go.

The system may change.

YOU remain. And that's where peace begins.

A person plays many roles: at home, at work, in society. Each role has its own system – rules, expectations, and feedback loops. But the person is not the system. The father is not the family system, the leader is not the organisational system, the actor is not the stage system. Systems are frameworks; the individual is the essence.

You are not the system; you live beyond it, and that distinction keeps you free.

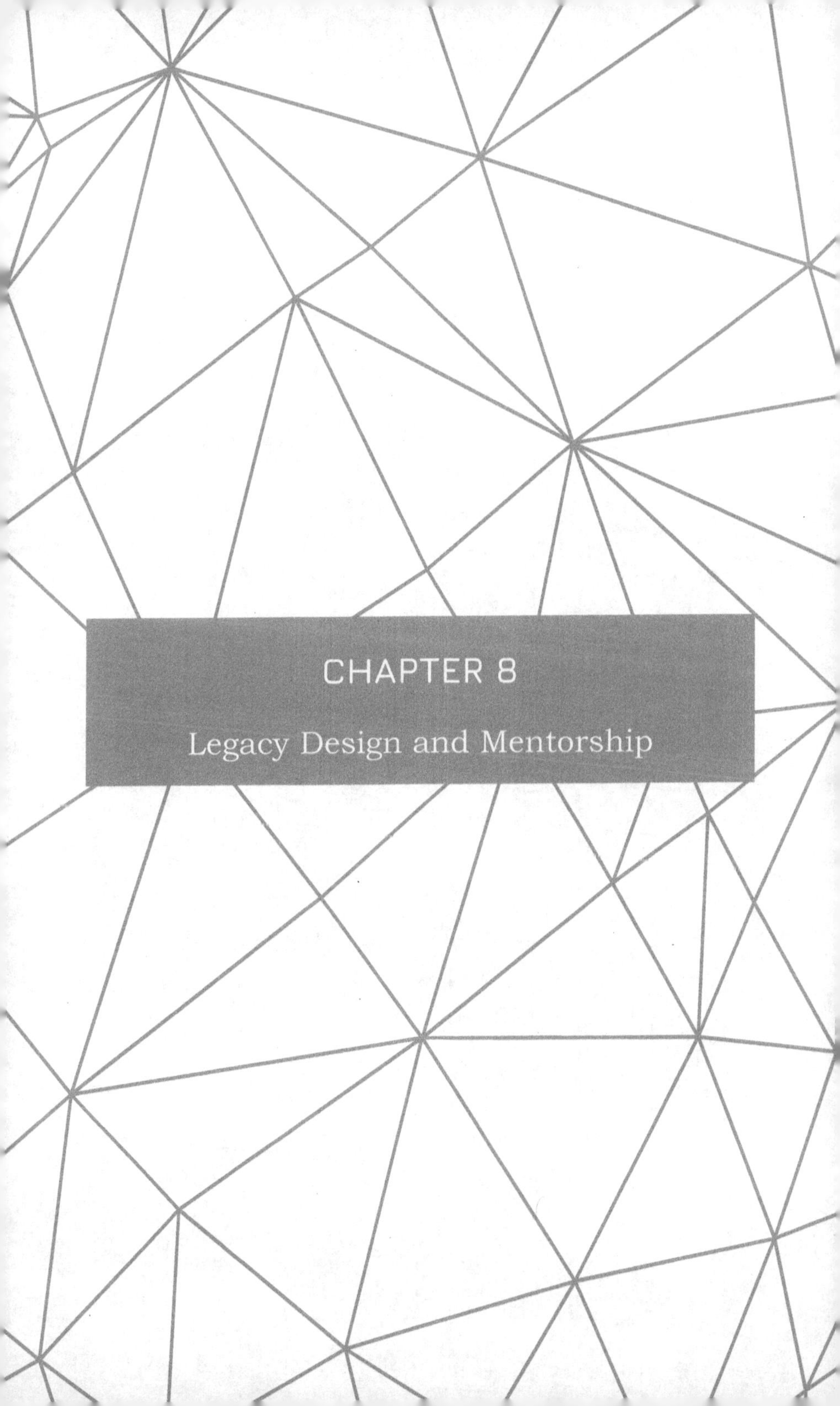

CHAPTER 8

Legacy Design and Mentorship

> Legacy isn't what you leave behind-it's what others carry forward because of how you lived

DESIGN FOR OTHERS

Systems are born when design serves beyond the self.

The best systems aren't built for the architect – they are built for those who walk through them. Ask: 'Will this help someone grow, heal or feel safe?' If yes, build. If not, pause.

Service is the soul of ethical design.

An Architect sketches the house. He thinks not only of walls and windows, but of the person in a wheelchair, who must enter with ease. This act of foresight is designed for others. It is how systems are built – by serving those who need and would live with dignity because of the design.

MENTORSHIP IS ARCHITECTURE

True mentorship designs space, not dependence.

Mentorship is a form of system design. You shape minds, beliefs and habits.

Every silence, every word, every question is a blueprint.

The ethical mentor builds with care, then lets the mentee walk freely.

In a martial arts hall, a teacher demonstrates a technique. The student repeats it, performing under his watchful eye. The teacher does not control every move; he designs the path, then lets the student walk it. This is mentorship as architecture: the mentor builds the foundation, the student builds the future. Systems thrive when mentorship is designed, not dominance.

LEGACY IS A SYSTEM

Legacy endures as a system – built to let light and life flow forever.

Legacy is not a moment; it is a system. It's the rituals, values and clarity you leave behind.

It's how people feel when they walk through what you built.

Legacy is an invisible architecture.

An architect designs a house. He ensures the pathways are clear, the garden nurtures growth, and the tall glass windows invite sunlight. Years later, the house still breathes, because the system was built to endure.

Legacy is a system; it is not just what we remember, but what continues to give light and life.

TEACHING WITHOUT CONTROL

Awakening happens when access is equal.

To teach is not to mould. It is to awaken. The ethical teacher does not impose – they invite. They don't demand – they guide.

The best lessons are the ones students discover

In this classroom, the teacher has chosen not to arrange her students in rigid rows. Instead, she places them so that every child can face her directly, with no one hidden at the back and no one privileged at the front. By treating each student as equally worthy of attention, she creates space for unexpected voices to emerge. Sometimes, it is the quiet child in the corner who, given equal access, discovers their own potential – and that awakening becomes the true lesson.

THE ARCHITECT STEPS BACK

True guidance is trust without control.

Once the system is built, the architect must step back.

Not to abandon, but to trust.

The actor will walk. The observer will watch. The system will breathe. That's when design becomes legacy.

A husband has taught his wife how to drive. Now, he sits beside her, not gripping the wheel, not taking back control, but offering calm support when she struggles. His role is no longer to command, but to trust – to let her find her rhythm while knowing he is there if needed. In that quiet stepping back, her confidence grows, and the lesson becomes more than driving: it becomes a design of trust.

CHAPTER 9

Observer's Compass

> The System may shift. The Actor may change. But the compass within you remains

THE COMPASS WITHIN

The observer is the compass that steadies the journey.

You don't need a map. You need a compass. The observer within you already knows the way. It doesn't shout. It nudges. It doesn't rush. It waits.

When you feel lost, pause.

The compass is quiet – but it's always there.

The observer stands alert, not rushing, not distracted, but quietly aware. It knows where to go and what to do, guiding both the actor and the architect. Just as a compass doesn't walk the path but points the way, the observer doesn't control or perform. It simply orients, ensuring that choices remain aligned with clarity. When the actor feels lost or the architect is overwhelmed, the observer's quiet direction restores balance.

QUESTIONS ARE TOOLS

Questions are the compass that guard clarity.

Before you act, ask:

Is this kind?
Is this clear?
Is this mine to do?

Questions are tools. They sharpen the architect's mind.

They protect the actor from confusion.
They keep the system honest.

A journalist sits with a notebook, not to chase headlines but to uncover the truth. Each question sharpens the fog, and each pause protects against confusion. Like the architect, the journalist knows that answers may shift, but the act of asking keeps the system intact.

Questions remind us that clarity is built not by certainty, but by curiosity.

STILLNESS IS STRENGTH

Stillness is the architect's quiet power.

Stillness is not weakness. Its strength. The observer doesn't react - it reflects. In moments of pressure – PAUSE. In moments of noise, LISTEN.

Stillness helps the actor move wisely.

It's the breath before the blueprint.

In a classroom, everyone rushes – typing, scrolling, speaking quickly. One guy sits still, eyes open, heart steady. He is not detached; he is observant. While others chase urgency, he notices patterns, pauses before reacting, and lets clarity rise. His calm is not escape- it is design. In stillness, he sees more than the noise reveals. That pause is his strength, the breath before the blueprint.

DETACHMENT IS DESIGN

The teacher's gift is to watch, guide and release.

To design well, DETACH. Don't cling to praise. Don't fear criticism. Don't get obsessed with perfection.

The observer builds, then let's go.

That's how systems stay alive – when the architect doesn't grip too tightly.

A young teacher guides her students, planting seeds of clarity. Years pass, her hair turns grey, yet she continues shaping minds with patience. She does not cling when they grow – she lets them walk their own paths. Her legacy is not in applause, but in the quiet confidence of those she once supported. Teaching is not about holding on; it is about lifting, releasing, and trusting that the lessons will carry forward.

THE COMPASS IS LEGACY

Values are the compass that guard legacy.

Your Compass is your Legacy. It is not what you build – It's how you build.

It's not what you teach – It's how you live.

Systems fade. Roles Change. But Clarity remains. That's what others will remember.

The medallion is engraved with words that have outlived centuries. The values do not fade with applause or time. They remain the compass, guiding choices when systems shift and actors change. The medallion is not a decoration; it is a reminder. Legacy is not built by noise, but by values quietly taken forward. When the architect steps back, it is these values that continue to protect, nurture and sustain the design.

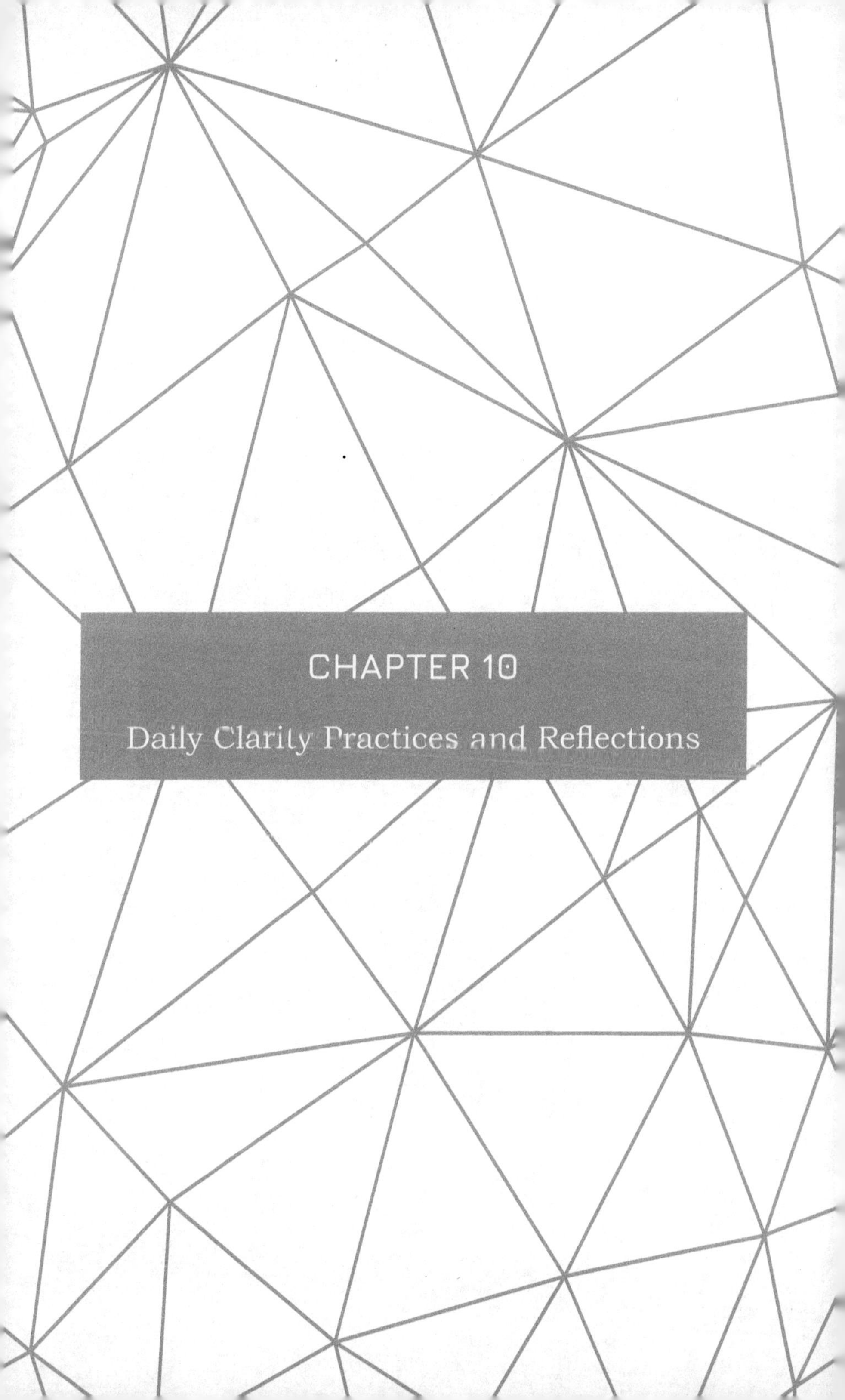

CHAPTER 10

Daily Clarity Practices and Reflections

> Systems are not built in a day - but each day is a system you can build with care

DAILY DESIGN PRACTICE

Routine is the architecture of the System.

Each day is a system. You design it with choices, habits and attention.

Begin with silence.

Move with clarity.

End with reflection. The architect doesn't wait for BIG moments. They just built the small ones.

A youngster wakes at dawn, journals, studies and reflects – day after day. At first, it feels ordinary, even invisible. But over time, the rhythm becomes a framework: choices align, habits strengthen, clarity deepens. What began as small acts now forms a living system. The architect doesn't wait for grand designs; they build through daily discipline. Routine is not repetition – it is creation. As the days pass by, rigour becomes rhythm, and rhythm becomes legacy.

THREE QUESTIONS TO BEGIN

Questions are the morning compass of clarity.

Start each day with THREE questions:

1. What matters today?
2. What can I let go of?
3. What will I build with Care?

These questions align the actor with the observer.

They keep the MATRIX (Maya) from creeping in.

As the morning light spills into the room, the young girl pauses before her day begins and asks herself the three questions. In that pause, the actor within her finds direction, and the observer within her offers clarity. The questions are not tasks – they are tools. They protect her from confusion, anchor her in rhythm, and remind her that systems are not built by chance, but by conscious alignment.

THREE QUESTIONS TO END

Reflection is the observer's gift to the day.

End each day with THREE reflections:

1. Did I act with clarity?
2. Did I listen to my Observer?
3. Did I leave something better than I found it?

This is how legacy grows – Quietly, Daily.

As the evening settles, a young man leans back, calm and unhurried. He asks himself questions – and the day's noise fades, and what remains is meaning. Reflection is not about judgement – it is about alignment. Each question closes the loop, turning ordinary hours into a system of growth. In this pause, legacy is quietly built, one day at a time.

YOU ARE THE ARCHITECT

Choice is the architect of the story we create.

YOU don't need permission. YOU don't need applause. YOU are already the architect. Every choice is a design. Every silence is a blueprint.

Every act of kindness is a system.

Built with Care. YOU are ready!!

At the table, a young girl eats quietly. Birds gather nearby, waiting, restless. She could have waved them away, claimed the space as hers alone. Instead, she breaks her bread and shares. In that moment, she does more than feed – she designs a story. Her choice turns strangers into companions, solitude into community. The architect is not always building grand systems; sometimes systems get shaped through small gestures. What she created was not just a meal, but a memory of kindness.

THE OBSERVER'S BLESSING

The observer is awake, guiding with quiet clarity.

May YOU act with Clarity

May YOU design with Humility

May YOU lead without Control

May YOUr systems Breathe

May YOUr legacy be quiet, kind and enduring

The observer within YOU is awake.

Let it guide YOU.

Even when the actor moves and the architect designs, there is another presence – silent, awake, watching. The observer does not interfere, but reflects what is seen: the pride, the haste, the moments of clarity. Its message is subtle yet steady. The observer is not the critic, but a compass. It ensures that legacy is not built on noise, but on discipline and grace. In its gaze, the actor finds restraint and finds balance.

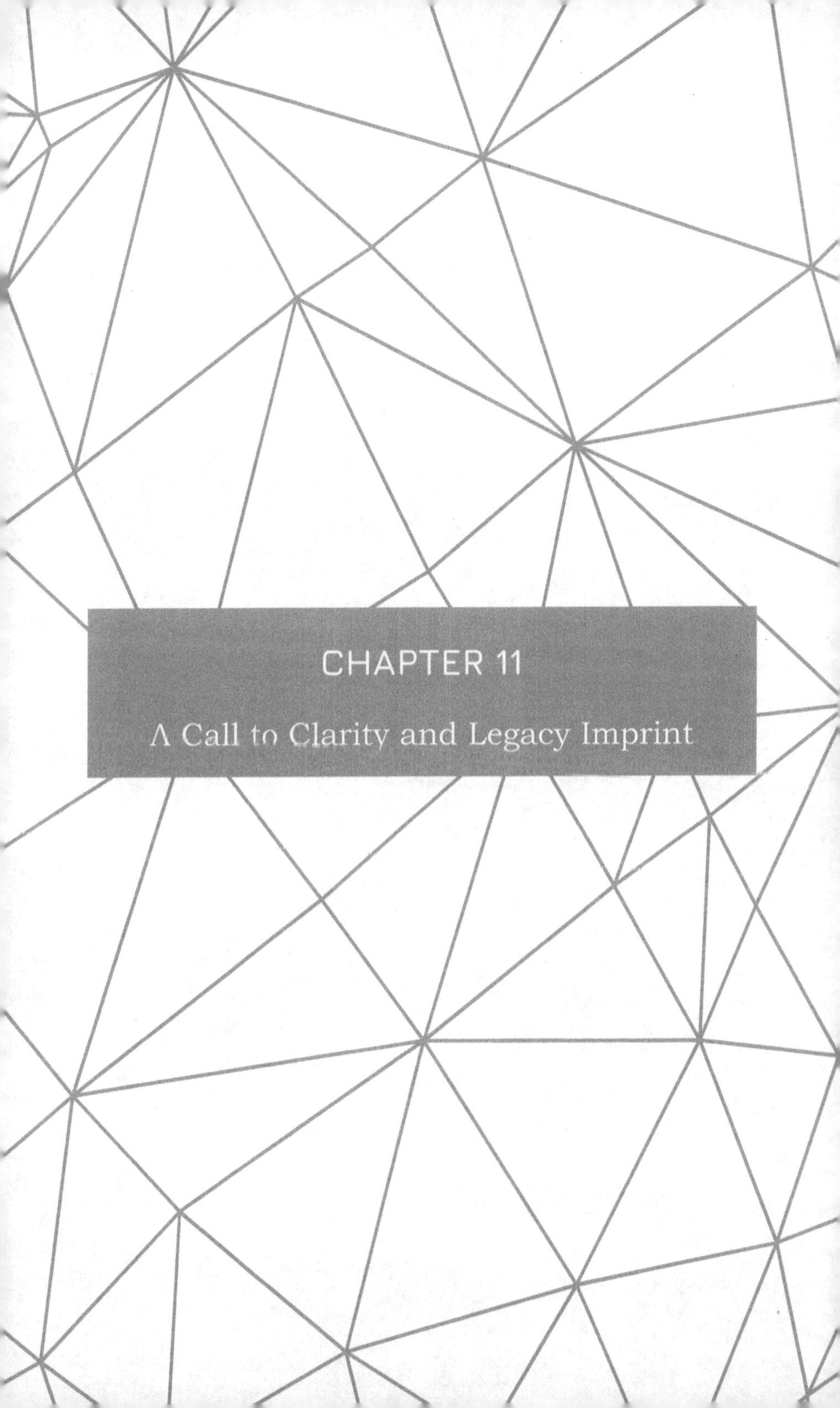

CHAPTER 11

A Call to Clarity and Legacy Imprint

The Journey ends where it began - with the observer quietly guiding the architect home

YOU ARE NOT ALONE

Every path is walked twice - once to build and once to persevere.

Every system you walk through has been shaped by someone. Now, YOU shape it too. YOU are not alone. Others are building quietly, observing gently and leading with care.

Find them – Walk with them.

An old man and a young boy walk hand in hand. For the boy, the road ahead is new, uncertain, and full of questions. For the old man, it is familiar – he has walked it before, built its systems, and left quiet markers along the way. Yet the gesture is mutual: the boy steadies the old man, and the old man steadies the boy. Legacy is not one-sided; it is shared. Every system was once created by someone, and later observed with care to ensure its integrity. In silence, the bond between generations becomes the compass – guiding and reminding us that clarity and humility keep the path alive.

THE MATRIX WILL TEST YOU

Clarity resists the matrix of urgency.

Systems will tempt YOU to perform, conform, and forget. That's okay.

The observer doesn't panic.

It Pauses. It watches. It remembers. YOU don't need to fight the MATRIX (Maya). YOU just need to stay awake.

A railway station hums with noise: footsteps rushing, voices colliding, trains arriving with urgency. Everyone seems pulled by invisible strings, compelled to move faster, as if delay were defeat. In the middle of this chaos, a youngster stands still. He watches but does not join. He knows the urgency is manufactured, the matrix designed to test his clarity. By remaining still, he avoids being consumed. The station becomes a mirror: systems will always create noise, but the observer's gift is to see through it. Clarity is not speed – it is restraint.

THE SYSTEM IS NOT THE ENEMY

Change is built through systems, not against them.

Systems are not evil.

They are just reflections.

Some are kind. Some are confused. Your job is not to destroy them. It is to redesign them. With Clarity. With Care. With legacy in mind.

A group of youngsters raise their voices in protest, restless and urgent. On the other side, others stand in line to vote – quiet, disciplined, purposeful. Both seek change, but only one channels it through a system designed to endure. The system is not the enemy; ignorance of it is. Protest without structure fades, but participation with clarity creates lasting impact.

LEGACY IS A DAILY CHOICE

It starts with a small act.

YOU don't leave a legacy someday.

YOU live it now.

In how you speak. In how you listen. In what you build. In what you let go. Legacy is not a random movement. It's a rhythm.

A youngster smoothens the sheets, folds the corners, and sets the bed in order. It may seem ordinary, but it is the first act of the day – a quiet victory. Done with care, it becomes more than tidiness; it is discipline, a signal that the day has begun with accomplishment. From this small act, rhythm builds and rhythm becomes routine. Legacy is not only in grand gestures – it is in the daily choices that shape clarity. The bed is not just arranged; it is designed as a foundation of a system.

THE ARCHITECT'S BLESSING

He steps outward to shape the world...
yet the mirror whispers: remember to reflect.

May YOU observe with Stillness
May YOU act with Clarity
May YOU design with Humility
May YOUr systems breathe
May YOUr legacy be quiet, kind and enduring
Remember
YOU are the architect and YOU are ready!!

A man stands poised, well-dressed, prepared to step forward. His readiness is not about appearance alone – it is the reflection of his inner architect. Within him, clarity has replaced dilemma, stillness has replaced noise, humility has replaced pride. He does not rush; he endures. The blessing of the architect is not a gift from outside, but the alignment within: actor, observer, and architect moving as one. In this moment, the launch is not just an act – it is a legacy. The architect's blessing is the assurance that clarity will always prevail, and the dilemma ends.

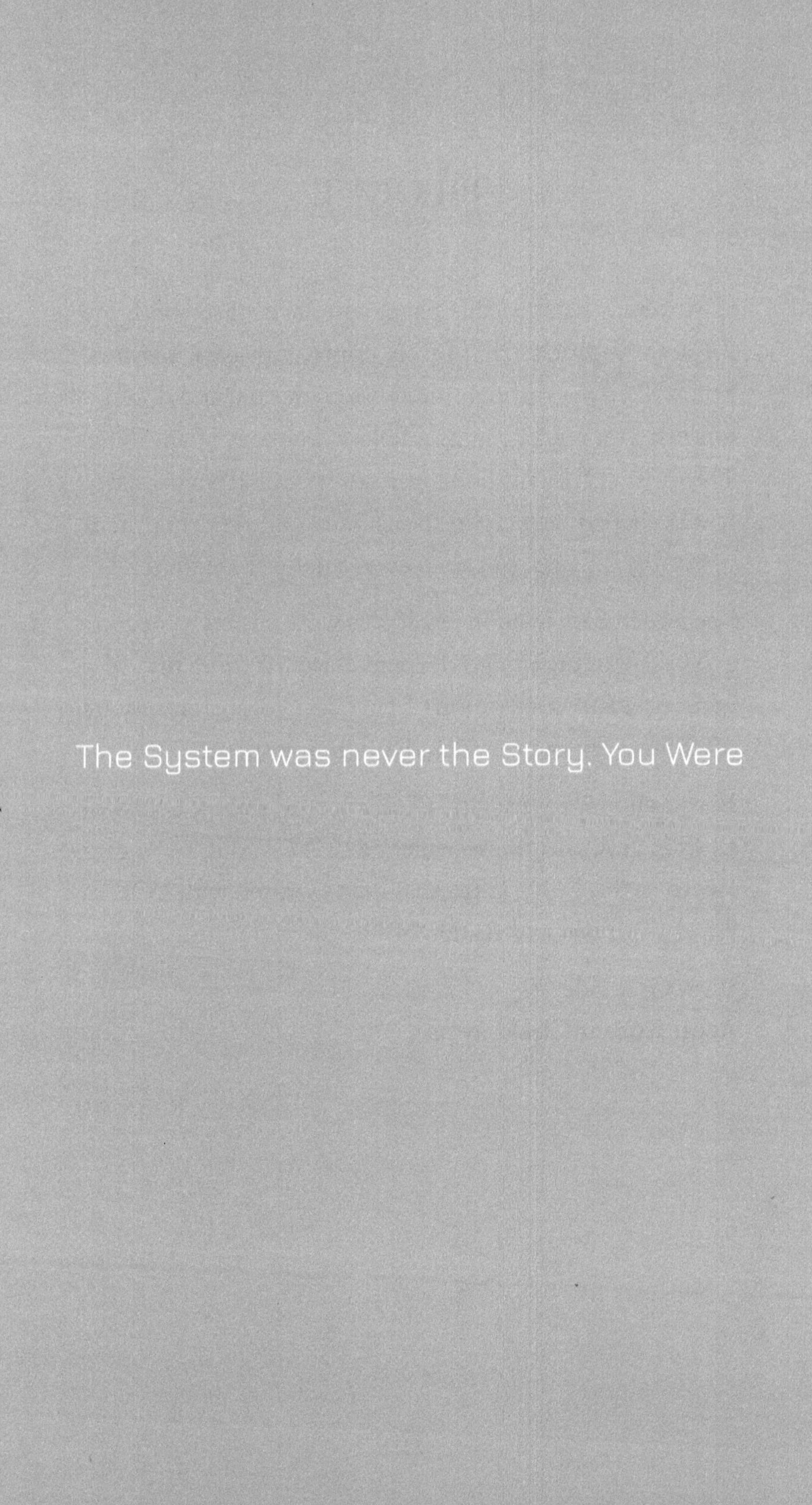
The System was never the Story. You Were

EPILOGUE

If you have reached this page, you have stayed with me through questions that rarely come with easy answers. You walked me through the tension, design, and doubt – not just as a reader but as a fellow architect of meaning. THANK YOU. This book was not written from certainty. It was shaped between responsibility and reflection. If it offered you pause, or peace-even briefly- I am grateful.

I believe in continuation. So, if this work stirred something in YOU – an urge to go deeper, slower or more inward – here are a few companions I have leaned on. They don't offer answers, but they ask the right questions.

If you choose to read any of them, read slowly. Let them sit with YOU. Let them challenge YOU. And if YOU ever return to this book, know that it was written with YOU in mind – not just as a reader, but a fellow steward.

With Gratitude,
Arun Kumar Chokkappa

RECOMMENDED READINGS

MEDITATIONS: A timeless guide to Stoic philosophy, Meditations by Marcus Aurelius offers invaluable insights into life, virtue, and resilience. This influential work offers a window into the mind of a Stoic philosopher-king as he reflects on the nature of the universe, the meaning of life, and the virtues that lead to a fulfilling existence. This inspirational read is a must-have for anyone seeking personal growth and enlightenment.

Almanack of Naval Ravikant: Getting rich is not just about luck; happiness is not just a trait we born with. These aspirations may seem out of reach, but building wealth and being happy are skills we can learn. So, what are these skills, and how do we learn them? What are the principles that should guide our efforts? What does progress really look like? Naval Ravikant is an entrepreneur, philosopher, and investor who has captivated the world with his principles for building wealth and creating long-term happiness. This isn't a how-to book, or a step-by-step gimmick. Instead, through Naval's own words, you will learn how to walk your own unique path toward a happier, wealthier life.

The Last Lecture: When Randy Pausch, a computer science professor at Carnegie Mellon, was asked to give such a lecture, he didn't have to imagine it as his last, since he had recently been diagnosed with terminal cancer. But the lecture he gave, Really Achieving Your Childhood Dreams, wasn't about dying. It was about the importance of overcoming obstacles, of enabling the dreams of others, of seizing every moment (because time is all you have and you may find one day that you have less than you think). It was a summation of everything Randy had come to believe. It was about living.

Vedanta Treatise: For those seeking answers on the purpose and ultimate goal of human life, this is an intensive answer. The Eternities: Vedanta Treatise is the seminal work by the author, and forms the core of the findings of over 60 years of research and study into the ancient wisdom of the Himalayas. The book expounds the ancient philosophy of Vedanta. It presents the eternal principles of life and living. Living is a technique that needs to be learnt and practiced by one and all. The technique provides the formula for remaining active all through life while maintaining inner peace. It helps one develop a powerful intellect to meet the challenges of the world. Above all, the Treatise helps one evolve spiritually. It provides the knowledge and guidance to reach the ultimate in human perfection. The goal of Self-realization.

Ego is the Enemy: Early in our careers, it can prevent us from learning and developing our talents. When we taste success, ego can blind us to our own faults, alienate us from others and lead to our downfall. In failure, ego is devastating and makes recovery all the more difficult. It is only by identifying our ego, speaking to its desires and systematically disarming it that we can create our best work. Ego is the Enemy shows how you can be humble in your aspirations, gracious in your success and resilient in your failures.

Thirukkural: A revered Tamil classic by Thiruvalluvar. It is a treatise on the art of living, composed of 133 chapters and 1,330 two-line couplets known as kurals. This work is highly influential in Tamil culture, celebrated for its universality and non-sectarian approach to ethics, morality, love, wealth, and politics.

The Alchemist: Santiago, a Spanish shepherd boy who leaves his home to find a hidden treasure at the Egyptian pyramids after a recurring dream. Guided by mythical figures and ancient wisdom, Santiago's journey becomes a profound quest to discover his "Personal Legend" – a universal destiny that connects him to the "Soul of the World". The story teaches that the true treasure lies not just in material wealth, but in the transformative journey of self-discovery and fulfilling one's unique purpose.

Do EPIC Shit: Ankur puts together the key ideas that have fueled his journey – one that began with him wanting to be a space engineer and ended with him creating content that has been seen and read by millions. His thoughts range from the importance of creating habits for long-term success to the foundations of money management, from embracing and accepting failure to the real truth about learning empathy. This is a book to be read, and reread, a book whose lines you will underline and think about again and again, a book you will give your family and friends and strangers.

The Monk Who Sold His Ferrari: is a revealing story that offers the readers a simple yet profound way to live life. The plot of this story revolves around Julian Mantle, a lawyer who has made his fortune and name in the profession. A sudden heart-attack creates havoc in the successful lawyer's life. Jolted by the sudden onset of the illness, his practice comes to a standstill. He ponders over material success being worth it all, renounces all of it and leaves for India. A visit to India about a spiritual awakening that opens up new vistas and Julian begins to view life in a different perspective.

The Matrix: the virtual reality world designed by machines in order to control the human race into believing it to be the real world, except for a few who have "freed" themselves and now struggle to free others.

BHAGAVAD GITA: The largest-selling edition of the Gita all over the world, Bhagavad-Gita as It Is, is more than a book. For many it has changed their lives altogether.

Universally Bhagavad-Gita is renowned and truly claimed as the crown jewel of India's spiritual wisdom. Spoken by Lord Krishna the Supreme Personality of Godhead to His intimate disciple Arjuna, the Gita's seven hundred concise verses provide a definitive guide to the science of self-realization.

SELF REFLECTION

SELF REFLECTION

Your System Begins Here

"Sit where you will... The reflection decides whether you are an Architect (Mind), Observer (Soul), or Actor (Body)."

IT ALL BEGAN WITH A DREAM...

I saw myself running madly, urgently- through a landscape shaped by fragments of my own thoughts. Words I had once spoken, ideas I had once held, now flickered around me like echoes. And then came the revelation: I was not just the one running. I was also the one watching. I was the architect of the dream, the actor within it and the observer beyond it.

This book was born from that moment.

It is a journey into selfhood – not as a fixed identity, but as a process. A way of choosing, shaping and witnessing who we become. Through reflection and recalibration, we learn to sit in the chair of our choice: the actor, the observer or the architect. The mirror and two chairs – placed at the threshold of the chapters and again at the end are not just symbols. They are invitations.

This book is not about answers. It is about creating processes – without losing your soul.

Arun Kumar Chokkappa is a debut author who has a Master's degree in Neuroscience from the University of Madras. His outreach is minimalist and deeply personal. He shares reflections on Science, Philosophy, Reading and Writing.

You can stay in quiet touch. This book is a beginning. If you would like to receive reflections, symbolic offerings, email: arun@teachingtaurus.com

'Teaching Taurus' is the author's imprint. It is a quiet space for the author's self-publication and soul-work.

HIT (Hear It Is) is the author's space on Spotify where he shares snippets of interesting text from literature that you can hear in less than 5 minutes.

www.ingramcontent.com/pod-product-compliance
Lightning Source LLC
LaVergne TN
LVHW090525110826
845146LV00003B/981

* 9 7 8 9 3 3 4 4 4 2 8 6 1 *